THE SWEATING SICKNESS

PITT POETRY SERIES

Terrance Hayes

Nancy Krygowski

Jeffrey McDaniel

Editors

THE SWEATING SICKNESS

REBECCA LEHMANN

University of Pittsburgh Press

Published by the University of Pittsburgh Press, Pittsburgh, Pa., 15260
Copyright © 2025, Rebecca Lehmann
All rights reserved
Manufactured in the United States of America
Printed on acid-free paper
10 9 8 7 6 5 4 3 2 1

ISBN 13: 978-0-8229-6738-5
ISBN 10: 0-8229-6738-3

Cover art: "The Abbess," from Hans Holbein's *The Dance of Death*.
Cover design: Melissa Dias-Mandoly

For my mother, Deb,
who taught me to see the world through the eyes of an artist,
and to speak my mind.

CONTENTS

Middle

End

Eurydice: I'm afraid!
Loud Stone: Your husband is waiting for you, Eurydice.
Eurydice: I don't recognize him! That's a stranger!
Little Stone: Go on. It's him.
Eurydice: I want to go home! I want my father!
Loud Stone: You're all grown up now. You have a husband.

Sarah Ruhl, *Eurydice*

Did he who made the Lamb make thee?

William Blake, "The Tyger"

THE SWEATING SICKNESS

Beginning

A DOZEN SONS

Say you have a dozen sons.
In the nocturnal forest
a dozen animals sniff
a dozen lilies hammered shut
for the night like flat
little bells like smells
to go in perfume bottles.
There is no moral to this story.
When a dozen boys run
through the night trees
they disappear between branches.
One of the boys is mine.
One of the boys is yours.
A brook crooks its way
through the dead trees
slicked with moss and fungi
pointing its finger to the east
where the sun will rise
a loose head on a string
or on a pike. One boy holds
a puppet and one boy holds
another boy's hand.
Why are my hands so sweaty?
asks a third boy. Four boys hold
down the corners
of the forest which they snap
like a sheet sending pinecones
into the air like hailstones.
One hides in a hollow log
one hides in a small cave
and the twelfth boy turns
into a lily turns into an animal
turns into a dozen pine trees
turns and vanishes in the night
ringed with a dozen stars

that are not stars that are
loose sparks.
Wouldn't you like to hold them?
These twilight sons
collecting in the forest.

NIGHT ELEGY

What was the night like when you slipped
a noose around your neck and leapt?
Did mosquitos hover in the fog?
Or was it clear, only the crickets' dirge,
a faint breeze on your cheeks?
Did you find Cassiopeia first,
trace her snapped spine with your pointer finger?

And your neighbor, when he found you,
hanged outside, as the sun rose
greedy-fisted over the bay—what did he see?
Did you waver? Did you sway?

Remember the way you demanded sex
and I gave it? The way you liked
to watch yourself in a mirror.
Who was the double you saw there?

When you fucked someone else
in the bathroom at a wedding,
I dropped a beer bottle in shock
and the glass cut a bridesmaid's
bare foot wide open.

The fighting, small slaps and pinches,
playful at first, became more pointed,
until one day you threatened to kill me.
You held me, firm, against a wall,
left a handprint bruise. Your spit
wet on my face. Your eyes
wild animals. Ruinous. Ruinous.

Once, I rode on the back of your bicycle,
shoeless, as you pedaled down busy city streets,
faster and faster. I clung to your pound dog chest,
and you screamed my name into the wind

and it hung there like a fading tattoo,
and it hung there, like you.

THE SWEATING SICKNESS

And so, the leaf of morning, pressed between
the window and the screen, the wild leaf
of autumn, as autumn itself, pressed between
panting summer and wet faced winter,
whose mascara runs in rivulets down wind-
pinked cheeks. And the lore of a bewitchéd
day, bewildered, as some lady, maiden,
peasant, throat slit, tied to a pyre
and crackling. *The sun rose, slit-throated,*
I once mis-translated from French,
when really it was *The sun rose*
over the trenches. Where is the rosy-fingered
sun? Busy with Odysseus, busy in
antiquity, on an agéd vase. Imagine
Calais, sweating out a summer fever,
the sweating sickness. Imagine Anne Boleyn,
sweating in a country palace, bodice
loosed, her virginity moldering away
as she waits and sweats and waits
and fevers, plague banner hung above
the fine wooden door, to warn off,
to ward off. Hang a banner above
your door, hang a flag, hang a sign,
as in the old days, when illness was
communal, when illness was realized
as communal. *I'm sorry my project*
is late, writes my student. *Covid has*
hit my house. Outside, the wind
hits the window, hits the brick
facing of the wall, hits the plain
wooden bannerless door. I hung
no banner when I coughed
through the night, when I fevered,
when my lungs inflamed and pussed,
when I checked and checked

9

and checked the pulse oximeter
and watched my oxygen levels waver,
waver. I'm no werewolf, and if I was
I'd work to hunt the devil,
to chase him, weaving, through
the streetlamps planted along the river trail.
I'd bite his tail and wail. No, I'm
no wolf, no witch, no lady waiting,
one hand on enchanted wood.
And if you place a witch bottle
above a fire until it bursts, I will not
howl and burn, as I burned, I will not
splinter into a thousand shards
of glass and rusted metal,
as a hex whispered in the night,
as a protective object buried
upside down before a threshold.
Inside, a woman lies gasping
cold fingered and splintered with fever.

SPECTER

What specter? This baby's love?
An extinct animal? Keats's ghastly
prismatic ghost-hand reaching
beyond the grave? My stepmother's
grandmother, now blind, head throbbing
as she labors to breathe, mouths
commands to a voice recognition software.
She just wants to see her family,
and not through glass,
and maybe not ever again.

A nurse spoon feeds her supper,
helps her to the bathroom,
tries to practice kindness through
her mask and plastic visor,
through her taped-on gown and gloves.
What specter? What eidolon?
What phantom? At night we watch
an actress dressed up as a princess
dressed up as Christine singing
"All I Ask of You" to her ghoulish
menacing husband who hates her.
She'll be a ghost in the next season,
when her car phantoms into the wall
of a Parisian tunnel in the spectral night.

We watch the fog sink in the graveyard
behind our house. In October
I walk through the back part
where the oldest graves are,
along the river, crying and snapping
morbid pictures of all the stones
that read *Baby, Baby, Our Beloved Babies,*

Mother & Baby, Our Beloved Infant Daughter,
Our Beloved Infant Son. How many graves
are from 1919, 1920, the last pandemic?

I weep on a stone bench, go home
and carve pumpkins into glowing skulls
with my children who ooh and ahhh
over their luminescence. There,
in the corner of mine eye, a ghost
go-eth, curly-haired, noose around
his neck, shaking his fist in my direction,
whispering *Dumb bitch.* In November
the deaths top a quarter of a million.
In December we lose and lose.

I run through the graveyard. What loose
pebbles slide beneath my athletic shoes?
What pointed leafless boughs snag
the bitter wind? What ghost? What specter?
What phantom? What fog? What
creeping miasma, come to carry
us Lethe-wards, come to sink and sink?

PAPER SKELETON VILLANELLE

You're as dead as the paper skeleton I hang
from my door. Dead as you, hanged man, cold clod.
Inside the house, my living husband and my kids

are rearranging time, and I join them, ticking,
letting go your skeletal hand. No, it's burned up.
No, buried and dead—your paper skeleton.

In an old photograph I see you.
You flicker into being. Inchoate. Negative image.
Inside the house, someone else's husband and kids.

We slow dance in the yard, amid the discard foliage.
You're dying to dip me. I lip your frozen breaths.
In death, your skeleton crumples like paper

in my palms. Your hands slip. I gather you up.
A bridal train. A black lace veil. Your ghastly sight.
Inside the house, my living husband and my kids

can't see you. They are busy with the light.
I push you to the gutter, filled with leaves.
You're dead as the paper skeleton I hang
inside my house, to entertain my husband and my kids.

YOUR LAST AUTUMN

In your last autumn
the leaves kissing
    the skeleton of ground
  you run to the end
of the gravel road
  well maybe not run
  limp and shuffle like
  a falcon whose wings
have been clipped
        who must stoop to walking.
        Why have I made you limp?
You didn't have a limp
you weren't even old.
      It would have been better
        if you had been.
      In autumn your ghost returns
but in your last autumn
      you got drunk and threatened
      to kill more than one person
        tho not me but I do remember
when you did and I do
        remember when I hated you
          and I do remember when I loved you
      but I don't remember why.
        Where's an image for this poem?
        You the gelded horse who wanders
  off the farm and stands
  on the train tracks. There.
          You the bull who wanders
        off the farm and kills a matador.
    There. Where'd the matador
    come from? You the hazardous
  rocks that pierce the hulls
  of ships circumnavigating
    the peninsula we grew up on.

You the ships whose hulls
are pierced. I suppose
there's beauty there
in that terror
that stiff terror
of your last autumn.

NARRATIVE

Here's one for you. After you died
I dreamed you were a boy, watching your
mother die. I loved you in the dream
though I also loved it when you mother
shamed you. Someone should have. Is there
a story here yet? I cut my arm watching
demons scale the sky at sunrise. Nobody really
believes in demons but actually lots
of people do and you did. I don't. Do I?

I cut my arm on a horse's saddle,
I cut my arm when the bright light
blinded my horse, blinded me, and he bucked
me into the wall of the riding ring.
How I hated that place, how I breathed fast,
how I was afraid to go fast on the horse,
to canter. I did exercises to strengthen
my legs, which had wasted away. Was this
therapy? She did that to herself, you used
to say about me, and sometimes it was true.

I put stones in my pocket.
I put stones in your pockets so you'd sink
in the River Styx. That's not true. Nobody really
believes in hell. That's not true. Lots
of people do and you did too. I don't.
Do I? Hell is other people is a thing
people like to repeat. I used to want to put
your face on like a mask, to see
what it was like in there.

I imagine your body traveled
in the sterile back of an ambulance.
Or would it have just been the morgue truck?
I would have preferred if you'd been
carried out on a golden litter.
You may as well have been because
that's what I can imagine now.

A person sweeps your house,
sweeps out patchy logic.
In the fairy tale, a boy and girl get lost
in the woods then gorge themselves
on sweets and follow a trail of bird eyes
back to their Germanic cabin.
My grandfather had a round wooden
table with this story carved into it.
In the story I am the girl and I find
my way out. You are the boy and you
don't do as well, but you've been so mean
that for a while I imagine you deserve it.

The reflective-paint cross on the back
of the ambulance cast a shadow
on your still form. You believed in god.
You used to. You would have liked that,
the shadow of the cross on your body.
I imagine the gurney as glittered gold,
wound with roses. You would
have liked the roses. I imagine.

CAT COSTUME

As a treasured youngest child you are
the cold wet rocks
the anemic sky.
The gold belly of your Halloween costume
reflects the light of passing cars.
I shout to you as you run away
fake cat who's caught
a bag of candy
who sits on the curb and meows.
Later there are cookies
flat hand slaps
of dough on a pan
overbaked and spread
dead already.
Little boy scampering
your mama is gone
like a breeze
on a warm autumn day
like the stinging nettles
dry and fall away like you
when you jumped
and swung from a branch.
Autumn is a line of tourists' cars
meandering up this peninsula
then meandering back down.
Autumn is a boy
pushing his hair out of his face
dreaming of a canoe.
His heart is full of dead leaves
falling down from dead branches.
In winter there will be no leaves.
Snows that swallow ground
will take the leaves and the water
will turn to ice and take the fish. Winter
like this peninsula

is named for death
like little boys running
into the early darkness of autumn.
They won't come back.

MANUFACTURED AUTUMN LEAF HOLIDAY WREATH VILLANELLE

Behind the manufactured autumn leaf holiday wreath,
you imagined you could see me but you can't.
Inside the house, my husband and my kids.

You know what kids are, though you abandoned
yours. Not me. You are trying to see me
through the center of the fake leaved holiday wreath

though you are dead as the paper skeleton I hung
from it, dead as you, hanged. Imagine, you, cold clod.
Inside the house, my living husband and my kids

are waiting for me. Jackolanterns cave in on
themselves on my front stoop, heads goopy and decayed,
dead as the fake leaves faking sick on the holiday wreath

encircling my heart, sad loop of rusted color.
Autumn blows a breeze to skin your reaching hand,
while inside the house, my husband and my kids

sing Ashes, ashes. Take your hands off of me.
I really did love you. Just once, admit it. You're dead.
Not inside the house living as my husband, with my kids.
Dead as the manufactured nylon leaves. Dead as the real ones.

EXIT

One morning I woke up and you were gone
but I didn't know it yet. Someone was cutting
you down while someone else filmed a video of it
that they posted on the internet. I was eating breakfast
with my kids. I wasn't thinking of you.
Even then you would have called me stupid,
called this poem stupid, called me smelly slut.

In the stillness of quarantine, I cut ties with the night.
I spent a lot of time thinking of you, turning you
around and around, man on a string spinning
in a void. Man who chose his own exit,
who opened a door and left. On the other side
of the door, what? Old junky time. Old eyes in a pile.
The friend who went through a year before you,
gunshot blanking his face. When you are gone
you remind me of my old dead grandfather,
lost in the woods, huffing exhaust from a hose.

The meanest and truest thing I said to you
was you would kill yourself or someone else.
I said it. That was before you threatened to kill me.
This is the last poem I'll write for you, hanging man,
spindle drop, dirt clod, moldering specimen,
lacing guitar strings together to form a lasso,
gathering cocaine into a bouquet to shove
into your nose, fucking and angry. Your anger
like a fast storm on the bay, coming to get you,

then me. A do-si-do into the grave. A false step.
A promenade. When you dipped me, I felt
bones in my hair. I felt the absence space of death
ring my ears. I felt the glowering allure of someone
who hates me. Inside me, a wrong woman

drawn to the dark, stinking of pussy, naked,
flawed-up, big-toothed and screeching, breasts
sweaty and flapping. I hate her. I love her.

I pick her up as I put you down, lower,
down into your grave. She hoists the first shovel.
When I found out you were gone I threw up.
I sobbed. I imagined the twitch of your foot,
the sharp twang of your neck, the way your fingers
stiffened. I imagined night, coming
for you with her dark hood, with her cape of galaxies,
with her low voice rumbling, *Ok, Ok, give me a minute,*
with her chin full of stubble. I imagined that she
lay below your feet, a force to pull and swallow,
a way to be still. A stillness. I imagined a stillness.

I imagined the night, a single cricket's trill.
A shadow that took you. That held your hand
and helped you down. Watch your step. This way.
That took you over the bay, so there was stillness.
Stillness and the night, humid and bug riddled,
but cooling, the dew condensing on the grass below.
Stillness, halting your body's droopy sway.

TWO DOGS

In one story we are two wild dogs
        in the countryside having just escaped
        the execution of the aristocracy.
We hide our tails between our legs
        knowing we have supped on blood
dripping from our masters' faces
                onto their fine carpets and divans
                        knowing we enjoyed the sound
of our trim nails click clacking
        across parquet floors as we ran as we
bolted from the gory scene
        whining and bereft knowing nothing
of reasons or motives or what to do next.
        The thing with dogs is they heave
                and retch up yellow foam vomit
        on the forest floor as they flee.
                I am the girl dog and although I try
        to lead we get lost among trees whose branches
obscure the moon and constellations
        that might've helped with navigation.
        I can't find our way, another thing that I
        can't understand. Meanwhile you want
                to lap water from a clear river.
        Where will we find a river running like
        clear water from an iron pump?
        I chase you into an open field.
        Us, the last two dogs scrambling up
                a tuffet of dirt and grass
                        to howl together in sorrow for
        the moneyed class. Yes, somehow dogs are
        able to understand the reification of class
        and its necessary destruction and
                their howls are also howls of joy.
                Say all the rivers flood even the banks
        we scramble across having finally found

the river we searched for
so we could wash the blood from our fur.
Say the forests flood, whole low-lying plains
fens, bogs and peat, a batch of crickets
washed away like
time will wash away our stories.
The answer to one howl is another howl
ringing through an imagined glade.

MOSES

When we finished drinking
We listened to REM

I painted
The kids' toenails

In another state
People died in a number

Staggering
We knew was coming

For us
The days piled up

We ordered
A swingset

When the playgrounds
Closed we ordered

A toy baby bottle
We cradled

The babies
In our arms

I tried to hide
The tears

I choked out
In the bathroom

And all the birds
The birds

The cardinals
And blue jays

And eagles
That came flying

Out of hiding
I guess

I pictured
Our babies

In glitter
In sunlight

In caskets
Held as flowers

In baskets
As Moses

Sent down
The Nile

By his mother
Squatting

Alone
At the river's edge

Coaxing
Live, live

CHARIOT

If I have unmasked and uncaped
what remains? An over-sparkled
diamond? A jewel-throated
hummingbird inciting the air
to violence? A spring from a rock
an old man split with a rod
that gushed and formed a dead
acid lake? Nothing lives there,
or what did enters putrefaction
even the red algae skirting the shore.
Make the lake a sea. Even the chariot
tracks in its coral calcify then stand
at attention. And I am not in the center
speaking in tongues, trying to commune
with a dead god, a fiery shrub in each
clenched hand. Neither am I
in a golden flying machine unearthed
in an ancient tomb. Not either am I
a mastodon carved on a rock.
I am not representational art
nor a narrative arc. An old man
is coming to see me, shaking his staff
which is a snake which is a sword
which is a pillar of fire which is a polished
wooden branch with handle worn
and smooth. And each of the old man's
sandals goes Doom Doom Doom
as it spanks the loose red earth.

GET LOST SERENADE

Peel back my eyelids and kiss kiss. Leave a coin
on each plump cheek. In a time of quarrel
I became a fine quartz pendant on a leather string.
I became a quark. A quantum wiggle. A flinging speck
that pops and pulls through space. I couldn't
undead the day. Unstable and nonlinear, I unpredicted.
I kicked my feet in the river but noodled nothing.
No catfish the size of small vans. No lost men
in scuba gear. If once the river flowed backwards,
while birds disappeared, well so what. If once
the ground shook, the light in its pendant mount
swaying above the kitchen table. I was asleep then.
If I leave a coin for you it is because I love you
like the river loves its mud. No. It is because I am trying
to buy you. I am trying to pull you into my heart.
I was a mother once too. I suckled one baby.
I suckled two. I left fresh flowers in my children's
rooms, and a coin to bloom into better dreams.
In my dream I held your hand and we went to the river.
It was night. The air laden with tulip-scent.
Mossy rocks fringed the shore. I mean bank.
At the bank I pulled out two coins. I mean,
when we got to the river, I pushed you in. When?
When the river washed you clean. Your memory,
I mean. When you died, I mean. I mean, you floated.
On each eye I placed a coin. I mean a petal.
And in your froggy ear I whispered, *Get lost*.

UNMOORED VILLANELLE

I'll tell you I was not unmoored. I lived.
I left the house, and though I moved back in
I didn't stay. I married. I had kids.

I got diplomas, three of them, undid
his bankrupt stare. I loved, no sin.
I'll tell you I was not unmoored. I lived

with joy, planted a garden, wrote books. The lid
of time, of sky, of day, of night unskins
my staid thoughts. I didn't stay. We were just kids.

I cannot say I didn't sway, or never slid.
I did. Like a child's greasy hand, like twins
who stare, unmoored, across the sky. I lived

not thinking of him much, until I did.
Until he roped time in a noose, and: fin.
He didn't stay. Unmarried from the sky, a kid.

In the yard night blossoms grew and when
I plucked one it was his crooked grin.
I'll tell you I was not unmoored. I lived.
I didn't stay. I married. I had kids.

INQUISITION

If we start in inquisition, we start
with a boxcar trembling and tenuously
filled with wrapped presents,
we start with a grief-benumbéd
brain, with Death who keeps stealing
from us, with the field of lilies Death
planted themself. Put the presents there.
They are not for the living children,
they are for the field of the dead
where each lily is a fungal purple
that thumps a bass tone through
the night. Alright, bring in the clouds
rigged on strings that my daughter
keeps mistaking for the moon.
Pull the lever and watch them zoom
across the sky, blossoming into
phallic protrusions. There's a hitch
in Death's giddyap, in the sky,
in the train track, in the field
of rotting lilies, in the circle of stones
Death placed to find their way home,
clutching a spit of pomegranate seeds
and baby teeth in their putrid hand.

REVISION WITH SUICIDE AND OGRES

Out of breath, I pull a penny from each ear.
And what do I hear? The scrambling *scratch scratch*
of a peacock's talons? The eyes of the peacock's bright
tail feathers, winking? Or nothing? Never mind.
Never in a mind to do anything, I have in each hand

a rock I could throw through a window
to let in the suicidal night air, drunk with cricket song.
That's the first draft. In the second draft, the pennies
are on the table. An old man named Fritz bends over
from his barstool and pulls a cigarette from behind

my ear. I'm four and wearing roller skates
inside the country tavern my parents spent
their last borrowed money buying. It's the middle
of the day and they must be fighting though I can't
remember that. *Scrub scrub scrub it clean!* says the ad

on the little TV atop the bar. The third draft
is a blank sheet of paper. The third draft will always
be a blank sheet of paper. In the fourth draft
my son is about to turn five. *Why is six afraid of seven?*
he asks. *Because seven ate nine.* In the fifth draft I

am in the fifth draft. I'm five. The bedrock
of one day then another cracks. Am I still
anyone's most precious thing? At school,
I do workbook after workbook to focus
on something else. How many suicidal peacocks

are at my young grandfather's funeral, dragging
their rainbow trains between the gravestones?
How many ogres, hairy and angry and reeking
of carbon monoxide and liquor, banging their fists
into the church walls? How many dead-eyed unicorns

lay their horns low? My parents must have been
there too, though I didn't see it. I was kept away
for my own good—good, good, goodness, be good,
be goodly. I wasn't there to see him lowered
into the ground, forty-seven years old and dead

by his own hand, with absolutely nobody
beating a penny into each of his senseless eyes.

Middle

A DOZEN DAUGHTERS

In the morning
in the twilight
say you have a dozen daughters
with full skirts sewn from pine needles
flattened galaxies and fox musk
little mushrooms stuffed in their pockets
to drop into a dozen creeks.
Did I say creek? I meant brook
which is more poetical.
The daughters stand in the brook
cold feet gripping at the mossy stones.
One of the daughters is mine.
One of the daughters is yours.
One of the dozen brooks
is full of minnows and crayfish.
The brook slashes the forest.
Four girls squat at its bank lifting rocks
to send the crayfish scuttling to catch
the crustaceans in open hands.
One girl pulls a pincer off and waves it
in the midst of all these trees
like a flag of victory. One girl wonders
from deeper in the forest she looks
down the galaxy line of the trees
and wonders about the branches
assembling like shaggy ghosts
like a dozen daughters flying
through the trees like bad intentions.
I know you want the daughters
to add up to twelve
but they won't. One turns
into a hollow log one
turns into a small cave one
turns into a blinking satellite
bobbing across the sky. That leaves five

daughters scattered like ashes like
embers in the dead brush.
Wouldn't you like to stamp them out?
These morning daughters
waiting to ignite.

CABIN

In the night, in the jeweled night. We scrape the jewels
behind the bed. Look! The stars we scrape across the night,
behind the bed, the stars like a million white ants in the sky.
Look! The bear dipping its paw in the bay. Look! The mossy rocks
we scrape our feet on, water shoes slipping from our pale soles.
The stars, the jewels, the sky, the bear, the woodpecker in his solitary work,
staccato-ing the day. Dot. Dot. Dot. Dot. Each dot a jewel.
Each jewel a bear. Each claw a jeweled hook that rests
upon the night's cheek, doesn't push in, just so, gentle jeweled touch.

Gentle jeweled throat. Dot. Dot. Dot. Dot. Each dot a slick rock.
Each dot a quick fish. Each dot a peasant festival.
Each peasant festival a fish, a bear, a jeweled mossy rock.
In the night, in the bear coated night. You put your hands
in its matted fur. Rake the stars out. Shake them behind
the bed like jewels, like a long stick to open a window
in a hot attic. A candle is burning there and the smell
of the hot wick and wax pins itself against the wooden walls.
It's stifling. It stifles. You open the window with the stick.

Let the stars in, their fish bellies shiny and sharp,
like all the memories we've forgotten, like the wet, mossy bears
that nuzzle the slick rocks and poke holes in the fish.
The stars cut your fingers, and your blood is a million staccato rubies.
Who built this house anyway? We were here to witness the sunset,
to witness the fish, to tap into the smooth waves of the bay.
There's a tempo here, a whoosh, whoosh, whoosh.

We are all the forest plants, hung with star shaped flowers.
We are the suicides of our friends. Dot. Dot. Dot.
We put on a record. We fetishize the antique technology.
We are digital but not. We are analogue. We are dot, dot, dot.
A bear rakes his muzzle across the night and stars wobble in their sockets.
They might fall out. What would we do then? We fill our lungs
with the smell of cedar and stars. Our children are nowhere around.

We are their absence. We are the cedars. We are pressed up against a cedar, making love, then, not. Dot. Dot. Dot.

SALT MARSH MOTH

I was held in place, a swamp moth,
shaggy faced, spotted and ugly,
a hot show, hot mess. Never very clever
I contra-stepped, contradicted, countered
with stoic wing-flap, leg twitch. I flexed
my thorax. Flexed? Is that right? Correct?
Accurately I was not without abdomen,
a place to pierce, a probiscis to don
a flower's flirty skirts, to phalange out,
long as a swan's muscled neck, mysterious.
I beat the chapped dawn back until
I couldn't. My multi-plated eyes,
they locked. The dim-lit, dimwit
tableau many tiles compounding,
forever stuck, a layering, a stacking,
a slough, all slag, a sloppy sludge.
And sorry I couldn't drop hindwing
and flee the gloved hand, take flight,
all fury and night bright. I couldn't budge.
I became a sculpture, static cast,
un objet d'art. With darting speed,
a quickness, in went the paralyzing pin.
It punctured. In and in and in, in, in.

MULE

In the distance
catastrophe crackles.

The lazy sway
of a swing.

The heartfelt
error. The ruby

held in one's
own mouth for luck.

Thanks Logic
with your rules.

Thanks Time.
Your tense

second hand.
Thanks Allegory

always a woman
riding nude upon

a noble horse.
A woman rides nude

upon a braying mule.
She is not pretty

or young. Her hands
catch the beast's neck.

Behind these meanings
another meaning.

Behind one child's
cough the other child

also coughing.
The *na na na na na*

na na na na of *Für Elise.*
I will always remember

the cough and the cough
and behind that more

like a naked woman
floating on the water's

greasy surface
like marigolds

like the dead.

BLUE

I saw the leaves and then the flowers
sprouting like crazed blue eyeballs
        off the loping vine that trellised
itself three sunflower stalks
and a late fall buttercup squash
        over the edge of the fence.
My daughter stood midframe
                in the photograph holding
a stuffed puppy and blue blossom
        blue blossoming off the bloom
                to midnight her violet shirt
        her tie dye leggings the color
                of afternoon sky. So few things
in nature are blue: blue jays,
        cobalt, the blueberry, nightshade
berries that shouldn't be eaten.
She was standing in front of
        a pile of dog shit
        telling me to pick it up, mommy,
                because she didn't want to step
in it and our real dog, not the stuffed one
        she held in the photograph,
had left it there. Those blossoms
        are not like crazed blue eyeballs
        at all they're like blue trumpets
        like strangled trumpets, choked
                off, oxygen needy, and inside
        ants crawl circles around pale stamens
just as the maggots she and I found
decomposing the walnuts outside
        her school worked their way
        through the earthy rind to expose
        the hard nut inside to help
        the daft squirrels gather and store.

PREDICTIVE MODELS

What if even the birds were recorded?
What if my husband was?
There he is, waving his hands over his head
signaling I give up, or Come over here—
I can't tell. What if poetry doesn't
mean anything, when compared to a refrigerated
morgue truck, to a fleet of morgue trucks,
to a pile of abandoned bodies
in a nursing home's small morgue.
Stop. My therapist says I need to learn
about mediums. What does that even mean?
Don't just stop things, she says,
but I have always just stopped things.
She wants me to listen to Brené Brown.
She wants me to write a poem through it.
Lol, I type in the chat window
when her call drops. I drink too much,
then I stop drinking. I don't exercise
at all then I exercise all the time. Lol.
Lol I type on my phone. Lol on Twitter.
When I was younger I was anxious
constantly. Stop. About what? It's May.
The projections are for 1500 deaths
a day. 31 times 1500 is 46,500 deaths,
a number I can't comprehend. We run
into the arms of the day and hope we're not
running into a morgue truck. We run into
the recorded birds. Their message is just
birdsong. Lol. It holds no meaning. A child
screams in the graveyard behind my house.
Her brother is chasing her. Lol I tell
the birds to tell my husband, busy reading
a book with our son. Lol I tell
the mean sober air. Lol. Lol. Lol.

IN MORNING

In the whale's spout, a rainbow.
In my daughter's hair, a rainbow hairtie.
In the holy, holy. Holy, holy.
In a diamond's carbon-sharp angles.
In each eye, a stone reflected,
a sore. Sorry I couldn't help you.
In each hand, a weight. Wait.
Wait. I am waiting for you.
In the plant's stupor as it turns
sunward. There's a word for that.
In the planet's stupor, carbon-spun.
In running across the field I find
the graveyard. In the graveyard,
deflated balloons, a collection
of ceramic rabbits, a pinwheel,
incense hangers and birdhouses,
a fastfood taco wrapper,
a child's lost black glove. Once
we spent a whole year at home.
I shoved a dog's face into the dirt
and growled, Down, down, get down.
I didn't want to do that, didn't mean to.
In the morning I am good, goodly,
I am trying to be good. In the tender
seagrass that bubbles and strings,
which I dream of. In my daughter's
footie pajamas, kicking against
my naked thighs as I sleep.
I have a tender spot inside me
though it is also electric and if
you touch it I vomit. That I exist
pushing light away from myself.
That I exist, a clutch of heavy bones
and I guess skin. In the narwhal's long
sensitive tooth. In its icebreaker,

echo-locator, tastebud and skewer.
In its pod behavior, its clannishness,
its looking out. In its deepest, blubbered plunge.
I have no suction cups. I have no unctuous
blessings. I have held the hands of nuns
but didn't mean it. In the morning
I want to head out early, stroke
a horse's muzzle, let her warm breath
tender the cold spots on my fingers,
tender my resignation from the night,
tender the frosted dirt, unstrewn
with little plastic parts. In morning
I go down the stairs and the day
is waiting. It is the same as yesterday.
It is a mighty sword. It is my dizzy
child spinning on the carpet.
It has shaken off its dead.
Spring is here and the day brushes
its hands together. All done.
There. In kindness. It is a kindness
to be done, to forget, to untie
the noose of death, the noose
of sickness, to look to the sun
and say, It is done. To the sun,
who doesn't care about us,
who doesn't care about
our dead. In order. It is over.
In a rainbow that is not a promise.
It is a kindness to be over, to be done.

NOTHING

I was the mayor
of no small city

no heavy bridge
no cauterized

desire. Powerless
and oblique

I shook like a fist
clenched beneath

a table like a jaw
clenched in the night

like the night clenched
against dawn.

Again, against,
I was raw

and reddened
and split

a contused knuckle.
I was small

as a crack on the bridge
of a battered nose.

I hollered
like the air

in the gap
of a car door

flung open on
the highway

mid fight
and I was the child

afraid in the back seat
back seat to

that chaotic love.

GHOST SONNET

When the portal opened, I didn't go in.
When I say "portal" I mean the treacherous strait
dusted with old skulls and shipwrecks, barnacles
and a half-sodden slim jim wrapper.
Lightning cracked the air. Water slid under the dock.
My throat, smoke-sore. All summer the fires burned.
My kids, out to their necks in the water.
Some ghost trailed me thru the forest,
fireflies and speeding car lights trying to shine
it out, like a stubborn doe, like an antler
you'd give a dog, like electric spiders weaving
a story into the night about a woman trying
to cross the rough-water strait while her brain bleeds,
the skeletal hands of lost sailors ferrying her over.

REVISION WITH MISCARRIAGE AND MAN IN THE MOON

When I had an abortion to end a miscarriage
I went under anesthesia, and I was grateful
for that, so I could wake up and cry alone
in the dark in my room, so I could hide
my grief. The darkness is the first draft.
The second draft is a transvaginal
ultrasound, administered at six in the morning
and in dim light. In the third draft,
there is my husband again. He is on an elliptical
trainer at the gym. He is lying in bed because
his hip hurts. He is carrying our daughter
while making sales calls, saying "I'm sorry,
you'll probably hear my baby on the call—
she's home sick today," to whoever's on
the phone, which is a lie he tells everyday
because we can't afford to put her in daycare.
In the third draft, there's a gray Midwestern autumn.
In the third draft, there's a barn that's been
bisected by a tornado, but still stands,
big gap in its middle like a missing tooth.
In the third draft I can't wait to eat
the pumpkins I've bought and lined
on the windowsill as festive decorations.
In the third draft, there is my husband,
dressed as the man in the moon. We're standing
on the side porch of someone's apartment
at a party sixteen years ago. I'm wearing a pair
of Groucho Marx glasses, tracing constellations in the sky.
The dark sky messed with stars is a draft,
is the first draft, and not the draft that ends
with me in a hospital bed, while a man in a Halloween
surgical cap shoots quick medicine into my IV line,
dances a little and sings "Monster Mash,"
tells me to count backwards from ten, nine, eight.

ABLATION

Whether the best method to staunch heavy bleeding is uterine ablation.
Whether pastel hued dream flowers in a hunter green dream field.
Whether the pills to reduce bleeding taste like nothing, just air.
Never, never, never, never, never, bemoans King Lear,
beholding a mess of his own making. Dear Reader, do pity him.
Whether the lightning strike of the ultrasound wand. O where, o where?
Whether the little dog turned away from the center of town, collar frayed.
Back into the illuminated room of today, hands braced on the doorway.
Whether dilation of the cervix is painful. If you've already given birth, maybe not.
Whether you gulp and gulp and gulp air before flip-turning against the pool wall.
Before I had a D&C to end a miscarriage, I daydreamed about taking up running.
Whether I wore a paper gown that inflated with warm air. The absurdity.
I don't even like to run but I suppose I wanted to run away
though the pregnancy was nonviable, had become life-threatening, etc., etc.
Look, a happier memory is me in a hospital bed cradling my newborn son,
then me in a different hospital bed cradling my newborn daughter.
Whether pastel dream flowers encircle those moments.
Whether time fleets, fleets away. It does. It scampers, flower-footed.
Whether the bells of the church down the street are always marking it.
Mark me, I will not buckle like a carbon-heavy star.
Nor am I a giant tortoise, laying mineral-shelled eggs in a sandy hole.
Look, said the doctor, it only takes a few minutes to put in an IUD and then it's done.
Whether the hormones affect only the uterus and ovaries and not the brain.
Whether I will swim across the wide bay. I am training and training to do it.
When the D&C was over I woke up. A woman told me I'd bled a lot,
gave me antihemorrrhagic medicine and a peanut butter sandwich.
I watched Jeopardy! on the hospital TV and couldn't answer any questions.
My mother was gone with my son. My daughter wasn't born yet.
Whether at least one of King Lear's daughters was having her period.
That's not in the play, but it should be. I had three pregnancies and my uterus gave up.
One of my grandmothers had eight babies and the other had five,
and both of them lost a child in infancy, clotted names no one repeats.
Whether my Catholic employer covers birth control. You have to say it's for heavy bleeding.

Just try the rhythm method, a doctor told my 1960s grandmother when she begged for the pill.
Whether this poem is a cycle, a circle. The inside of my uterus is hunter green, I imagine.
Each fat clot is a pastel dream flower, rooted in sloughable walls.
Whether walls imply a room. What type of room can expand and contract?
Whether my congresswoman passed a fetal remains bill. What the fuck is her problem?
She is a holy-rolling evangelical, pious-faced woman and I don't even believe in god.
This poem was always already political. In dreams, I pick the brindled puppy
from the litter, but I don't like dogs, their wild, percussive barks.
Whether I eat an iron rich diet to replace the lost blood. I better.
I like to float on my back in a large, cold bay and dream about quietude.
Where are the tall, hunter green pines fringing the harbor?
Whether the bay gulls fly in a low circle above my womanish form.
When they open their beaks, bouquets of pastel flowers ascend into the spheres.

BLOOD MOON

The Earth flips like a coin in the sky
seen through the lens of a telescope
set up in the driveway of a boy
on some other planet or moon
our moon maybe or Titan or red Mars.
Let's go to the Underworld!
my son exclaims as he builds a fort
with his sister whose name
is Zephyr not Persephone.
They dive between the pillows
and propped up blankets.
Zephyr means a gentle breeze
I tell my daughter. Not a gale.
In November gale force winds
sheer the top off an old pine
in our backyard. The treetop slams
to the ground while we're feet away
tying a tarp down on the fence
we share with the graveyard.
Snow falls the next week
and icicles hang daggerlike
from the eves. At a dark hour
I wait with my son for the bus.
We get out his telescope and gaze
at a red lunar eclipse blood moon
or pink moon as my daughter
calls it when she wakes up
and puts on her pink rainbow
coat to join us in the cold
and look through a set of lenses
at the shadow clad orb.
A fox holds a heart
in the ornament hanging
in our front window
which catches the bloody light

of the moon sweeping over us
in the early morning over the snow
over the icicles over the downed tree
over my neighbors who pull
out of their garages and drive
to work never looking up.

THE RED PLANET

The child dreams a door, in the distance.
The distance is a metroplex theater,

each screen playing a different film.
No, the distance is a hand with brittle finger-

nails, one chipped. No, the distance
is a planet. There on the planet, a door,

a portal. The planet is the child's
round head, collapsed on a pillow.

In his sick bed, the child pants and moans,
asleep but still suffering, fever

spiked and a metal bowl set
by his bedside in case he vomits.

Wouldn't that child like to go through
the door on the far away planet?

With his pale hand he might open it
to find an elephant, a whole herd

of elephants, stomping through the red
dust that is characteristic of the planet,

for which the planet is known, stirring
it up in big, blood-colored dust clouds.

Or, he might find a theater, totally empty,
no one in masks, playing his favorite

superhero movie, the one where the hero
saves the red planet from a black hole

hurtling through the multiverse. He might
find a poem, written by his mother, left

on his pillow. The poem is a limerick
about the child's dog attending

a birthday party filled with red balloons,
red as the child's cheeks, hot with fever.

The child tucks into a curled ball
in bed, like an alien on that other planet

might curl its armored back to form
a protective spiral shell. Spiraled,

like the dreams of the child,
which corkscrew around the red planet.

Spiraled, like the whorled beats of my heart
as I watch over him, check his chest

for steady breaths. Spiraled,
like the curled arms of a wide galaxy,

galloping across space, cradling
the dusty red planet, cradling our own,

in its proton-heavy arms,
in its star-hot arms, in its comet-pocked arms,

cradling the sick and dreaming child.

ABORTION POEM

I want to write a poem about abortion.
I'm driving to Rural King to get a key cut.
I'm in rural Indiana. Then I'm in rural Michigan.
I'm in Michiana. I'm driving to Niles.
I pass the neon Pegasus sign outside a gas station,
always off. I pass a man panhandling at the intersection
of two rural highways; one of many men panhandling
at many such intersections in Michiana. It's 9:00am and already
85 degrees and he's in the shade of the telephone pole.
I pass Galaxy Skate, whose sign is a giant pair
of roller skates with wings, like Mercury's shoes,
like golden Nike. When I was a child,
I roller skated around the ballroom of my parent's
country tavern. I roller skated at a rink whose name
I've forgotten. Every time they played Van Halen's
"Jump" all the skaters would jump in time to David
Lee Roth's exhortation: "Jump!" and a couple dozen
skaters lifted off the rink at once, a couple
dozen skates slammed back into the shellacked cement
rink, overlaid with a glow-in-the-dark galaxy tableau.
"Jump!" and we'd jump together. "Go ahead and jump!"
and we'd jump together. That was in a different state
tho, not here, not in Indiana, not in Michigan.
I'm on my way to Rural King, which is like Fleet Farm,
which is like Tractor Supply Store, which is like Farm N
Fleet. All of these stores sell baby chickens in spring,
display bright vinyl banners that read "Chicks Are In!"
and I take my children there to see the baby chicks,
which we can't pet because they're not pets, they're
for laying, they'll be laying hens and then they'll be
stewing hens. They're for food, not for fun. I should
take my children to Galaxy Skate, to see if it's painted
like a galaxy inside, to see if it's got neon glow-in-the-dark
paint, to see if we might disappear there, in the darkness,

only the lightest parts of our clothes, our teeth, our eyes
glowing in the black lights. At Rural King the key cut machine
is broken, no it's turned off, no it's unplugged, because someone
was vacuuming and forgot to plug it back in. A guy with a ponytail
helps me turn it on, helps me select the keys I need. I make
a mistake and accidentally select four copies, and by the time
I realize it, it's too late to go back. The machine slugs along,
copying, copying, copying, copying. One key has Captain America
on it, and the others are brass, with the Minute Key logo
emblazoned on their heads, and I've been waiting a while now,
ten minutes, fifteen. Finally, I collect my keys. I'm leaving
Rural King. I'm leaving Niles, Michigan, to drive back
to Indiana. The sides of the rural highway are littered with trash.
Some of it sparkles. What happened to my poem about abortion?
It's the 22nd of June. In a day or two or three or a week,
the Supreme Court will likely strike down Roe V. Wade.
I had an abortion six years ago. I was 35. Do you want
to know the details? Of course you do. My pregnancy
became life threatening, became nonviable. Does it matter
that the pregnancy was wanted? That my OB said, "This is an abortion,
not a termination?" That it happened in a hospital, with full
anesthesia? That it happened in New York? If I had lived
in Indiana then, would I have been asked to miscarry naturally,
despite the life-threatening nature of the failed pregnancy?
In the car, I'm listening to The Smashing Pumpkins. "1979"
comes on, and I remember listening to it on the school bus
in the nineties in rural Wisconsin, wearing blue lipstick,
a shiny neon dress, sparkling glitter tights, platform shoes,
the music on my headphones cranked up to drown out
the bus driver's country radio station. In the nineties
everything seemed possible. Was it the decade or was it
my age? The hopefulness of youth? The country would get
more progressive, I thought then, not less. If Roe is overturned,
abortion will be illegal in Wisconsin. It will be illegal in Indiana.

It will be illegal in Michigan, though the governor there is trying
to do something to keep it legal, and if she succeeds, I'll move
to Michigan. I'll move to Niles. I'll shop at the Rural King
and skate at Galaxy Skate. Or, if she doesn't, I'll quit my job and move
to Illinois, one of the only Midwestern states that's pro-abortion,
that is enshrining abortion into law. Because I am afraid of travel bans,
of being arrested for leaving the state of Indiana to get an abortion,
or of my daughter, who is three, being arrested for leaving the state
to get an abortion in 8 or 9 years when she gets her period,
when she could be raped and impregnated against her will,
and I know Indiana won't have an exemption for rape,
or for a child being pregnant. And I hate that this is making
me think about my only baby daughter being raped, being a pregnant child—
I hate the violence of that. Here is the abortion poem,
and it's no longer very poetic. Here is the story of my family,
which is just one family among many, and I don't mean to be dramatic,
but a fundamental part of my rights, and of every woman, girl,
menstruating person's rights is about to be taken away.
And now I'm back in Indiana. I'm driving past my children's
summer camp, past the Catholic college where I work.
If I publish this poem called "Abortion Poem,"
will they fire me? Then I could leave Indiana. Then I'd have
an excuse. Over breakfast, my son asked me why my grandmother
had so many children—eight children. And I said, without thinking,
"Because birth control was illegal then." Tho I could have
also said because abortion was illegal. As it's about to be again.
"The street heats the urgency of now," Billy Corgan's voice blasts
from the speakers in my car, "As you see there's no one around,"
and when I get home I play the entire album on my backyard speakers
as I sit in my kid's little kiddie swimming pool in my one-piece swimsuit,
trying to outlast the heat of the day, of this umpteenth day in June with 100
degree heat. I play "Bullet with Butterfly Wings" and scream along when
it gets to "Despite all my rage I am still just a rat in a cage"—me, a forty-year-old
woman sitting in a plastic pool in her backyard, like a child, like I did as a child.

Let the fascist neighbors with their blue lives matter flags hear me,
let the priest in the rectory down the street, let the ghosts in the cemetery—
they've had enough peace. Let me have the strength, when the ruling
comes down, to know what to do next, to know what to do
with my hot, angry heart, whose beats sound like Fuck you. Fuck you. Fuck you.

WHEN THE WIND BLOWS

The fallen basket of crab apple blossoms
dusts the yard in pollen, in petals,

like confetti. Inside the basket a daughter,
a snake, maybe, a rabbit. I sing

to the tree's broken bough, rock-a-bye
winter, the end of hard-edged time.

Pretend you can't find me, my daughter
says at bedtime. Pretend I'm high in the tree.

Under a blanket she sticks her arms out
like branches. In the early dawn an eagle

swoops low in our yard, looking for prey,
a rabbit or vole, maybe a snake. She circles

the school bus, yellow accordion door
closing behind my son, who is crying

because he's lost his ID badge again.
The wind blows and rocks the bus,

rocks the boughs on the half dead trees
lining the yard, rocks the eagle on her hunt.

In her nest her mate shelters a pair of bald eggs,
waiting for food. Imagine the burden of circles

she swoops by the river—that muddy worm—
hunting for crayfish, exhausted and hungry.

The river puckers into small waves, kisses the air
beneath her talons. The air is a basket

I could climb into, like a nest, a bed, a blanket,
the bough, like an eagle, like light,

my consciousness split into petals and rocking.

TRAIN VILLANELLE

You've lost a penny, you've lost many, you've lost your brain.
My son traces a maze with his finger, one
leg kicking under the table to the tempo's fast train.

Leave my son out of this. Smiling boy who frames
his pictures with stickers, not yours to touch. Be done.
You've lost a penny. You've lost many. You've lost your brain

of course because you're dead, can't think, can't blame
anybody else now. Now, I want you to go,
skeleton legs running like a cartoon train.

Skeleton key in freeze frame dangling from your sprained
neck. No, broken. In the tarot deck you're upside down,
a lost penny, discarded man with sloshing brains,

your head hinged to ground, one foot flamed
to the side, untied. Delirious spectacle. An eye to thumb
shut. A punch of stars. A halo or arrow, untrained.

I flip you right side up again, spin and spin
you. I'm in control, blow and the boughs
break, like your neck, like a baby, lost, like your brain.
Like your legs twitched a slow tempo, then stopped. Then stop. Then stop this train.

NIKE, MEDUSA, JOCASTA, SPLIT

When I speak in my most heretical voice,
he will know. When I come with my hair
undone—no, taken off—no, on fire—
no, turned to snakes. A woman in her power
is a woman creeping over a finish line
bloody kneed and gasping for air—
no, is a woman levitating—no, is not
a woman at all, is a high-pitched wail
echoing through a dell lined with bats
who shriek and fill the night and gobble
squirming larvae. At the end of one's
rope there is squirming, at the end of one's
tether. When I wrote about him
I wanted a cheap trick for a poem;
I didn't imagine he'd come back to life
and breaststroke through my dreams.

He was always froglike, delicate,
a specimen to pin down with his doctored
nose, his fluttery lashes, his slender-
muscled arms that batted and batted,
even his penis, cocked and loaded
with gooey pale semen that never
got me pregnant, that I spit
in a dirty toilet. Done. In my most
heretical voice I flay him
and dissect. I raze the house
where he threatened to kill me
and build something else—a temple,
a glass greenhouse, a single room
where I wait with wingéd anticipation,
each hand holding a hairpin
to shove into his eyes, each hand
holding my anger, destructive. Except
he's gone. Hanged and buried.

Eyes stitched shut so no light
can find them, not even the sickly
morning light through a long-
demolished window that once,
when we were young and drunk,
tumbled across our sleeping backs.

There was no love there. Or,
there was all of it. I don't know.

TWO LOVERS

In one story we are two lovers
scrambling up the banks of the Rhine
a river I've never been to
that I've read stories about
in the way working class people
read stories of the affluent
vacationing and fucking and betraying
their own brothers and stepping in front
of trains that have come loose
from their tracks and instead of brakes
have two sad faced women
waving kerchiefs from the railing
of an old caboose.
The thing with rivers is they crook
and bend sometimes they are tidal
and I have spent a lot of time
writing about them.
I thought our lives would crook
and bend but mostly they
are just the day to day
which you excel at and I
am bad at. A woman wants
to meet me in Chicago.
A train is waiting for me.
I chase it down the tracks
use my kerchief to catch
the railing of the caboose
to hoist myself onto the little balcony.
The woman is already there
disappointed in me. My son
my daughter two sad faces
in the caboose's back windows.
Say we are climbing the banks
of the Rhine. This poem
a spiral, repetition with progress.

I hand you a glass of chilled beer
make apologies for things I can't
control. Next time, I whisper,
I will be a naked beauty
a face carved in a rocky cliff
the answer to a question
you haven't asked yet.

End

BOG BODY

A coin stamped with the face of a king
passes from hand to hand
like crystalized labor.
There are no swamps as deep as
ten kings' bodies stacked
vertically toe to crown.
Many ancient kings were buried alive
in the peat-bogs
screaming then disemboweled
some Earth Mother waiting for them
to sink into her gawping sulfur mouth
of reeds slowly over a millennium.
Zephyr is the name of a fearsome queen,
a gale that could pummel
a sacrificed king
half-submerged in a lowland fen.
In May gale force winds
sheer a comet loose from its orbit
in the starving navy sky.
In May a wind-sharp sword
sheers the head
of a queen right off.
Snow falls like burial trinkets
like love notes
pressed in the hand of a sacrifice.
Open the curtains to the underworld—
it is speckled with stalactites
speckled with bats
speckled with hungry mosses
to eat the bones of the dead.
Open the eyes of the doomed one in murky
sludge in a bronze diadem
to gaze no to stare as in a trance
at the sunrise drenched swamp.
In its toothy mouth

the bog holds a handful of pearls
pried from the sea
that it will soon ingest like a flood
of salt water ingests
sunk metal or a whole wooden chest
given enough time to pull apart splinters
apart molecules. A coin
stamped with a king's face clambers
in the chest's forgotten corner.

THE UNDERWORLD

Don't fucking look at me. I'm not here for you,
hobble-scotched, limping through the house,
child crying, always a child crying, in the background.

Even this daft dog, barking. I'm lonely
and nobody listens. Listen. Listen, I said.
Then I stopped saying. I recessed. I grabbed

two sheaves of dry hair and pretended
to be a witch. I pretended to be the CEO
of a drug company selling the public

contin-coated morphine. Just take an 80mg pill.
Just take a 160. I pretended I was a queen
waiting to be beheaded by an impotent king

who couldn't even show his face at the trial,
who hid away with his new young lover.
Had the queen fucked her own brother?

I couldn't say, though I knew each stone
in the tower wall. I pretended I could raise
the dead. Who first? My friend, the addict.

My ex, the addict. My grandfather, the addict.
Go back down, down. Enter the underworld
on a leaky elevator, and who is there waiting?

Nothing. Nothing. Be numb. Benumbed, I did
not raise myself. I am no redheaded Plath,
gobbling men like hot oxygen, though I want

to be. I'm not scribbling limericks, trying to rhyme
dildo with mildew or tulip with cunt.
In the thirteenth month of the pandemic

I pressed my children to my breast, though I'm no
wolf come to nurse them. I'm no queen
of the underworld, either, though I too

long to disappear in winter, to go down
with the stones and secret rivers. I'm not a fluorescent
light or a light chime to signify nullification.

Be blank. Absent. Nothing. I'm not the dominatrix.
I'm not the lover. I'm not mooney Eurydice,
but if I was I'd say my Orpheus swung and swung.

He went down first. Gird the underworld
with tulips (with cunts). Gird it with crabapple blossoms
and a child who won't listen to me. When I am nothing

I will lie on the ground, eyes closed, and let
my grief fall from my feet like lead. As the dead were dead
and no one bothered to come. As I raised them,

then put them back, and said Don't move a muscle.
Stay put. Don't turn your head. You're dead.
You've always been dead. You're a hole in a rotten

man's head; a band of ligatures at his neck.
You're a tailpipe so hot it burns a brain right out.
You're the stars turned off. You're dead. Stay dead.

NOOSE

He was like the town bike
everyone got a ride. He was like a ride
that made me vomit. He was like the vomit
I spewed in a Wendy's parking lot.
He was like a parking lot I lay
down in and let the hail beat and bruise me.
He was like a bruise you discover but can't
remember where it came from.
What did you smack into?

By now you know his hands
were threats. By now you know
his hands were switches. He was like
the switching breeze that smacked
the chimes against my house the morning
I found out he'd hanged himself.

What else is there to say? I hung
those chimes. I hung his memory up
in the collective grief of the pandemic,
where it was small, where I could
convince myself it was small. It wasn't.

He was like the placid night bay we swam in,
naked, when I was a teenager and he was 25.
On the surface the stars' reflection,
the northern lights, but underneath muscles
whose shells could cut your feet to shreds.
My naked teenage body brushed his naked
man body. What does grooming look like?

On the phone with another man,
his friend, I comforted. I said, Put the bottle down.
Dry up. Take care of yourself. I put my own self
inside the smacking chimes. I put my own

panting, retching grief in there. I put
my stale hate in there. Grow up. Let it go, already.
I put my anger. My hot, justified anger,
sweating, breasts exposed, feral
and ready to tear out a throat.

I paced my yard. Upstairs my children
slept, unknowing. The breeze slapped the trees.
The trees slapped the power lines.
The power lines slapped the side of my house.

He was like a blister I picked,
hot, and inside the blister his shitty eyes, no,
his rubber nose, no, his fucked up laugh—
that fucking fuck—no, his hands that grabbed
and slapped and grabbed and smacked
and grabbed and pulled the noose tight
tight tight. T-I-T tight. He was like a noose
that shrunk and shrunk until it snapped
and disappeared, and I was the smacking branch
he hung from. No. I was the rope. No. I was inside
the noose too. No. I stepped out just
in time. No. I never could. Really. Really.

He would have killed me if he could,
and, Reader, whatever, he would have killed you too.

LEDA

I wanted to thunder and pull down
the sky, like a flailing swan pulls down
a wolf from the forest to bite its
long neck. If I had a long neck, like
a swan, a giraffe, an unsexable
woman. I spent all day in bed
exhausted and weeping. My bedroom
a riverbank, broad meadow, cavern.
The clouds in the sky hung like taffy,
so sticky. Their mystery gooey.
Or black crepe you'd hang for a funeral.

If I scraped my short fingers
across them they'd ripple and scatter.
They'd dissipate. God could be hiding
there if they existed. Their hair done
in cumulus poufs, their plain smock pinned
just so, with the branch of an apple
tree pulled from an orchard and jabbed through
the fabric. Control what you can, what
you imagine you can. In my bed
where I'll always be weeping, until I
turn into the swan. In a dream.

All my feathers will molt and will mark out
a path to the underworld, a path
to your grave. Where I imagine you'll taunt me.
A stone for each insult. I imagined
your face would be stilled, but it wasn't.
Your grave is a beach on a lake,
is the pines on the shore, is the pelican
swooping to catch a small fish, little
perch or small alewife. Your grave
is a lyre I could strap to my back. I
could strum all six strings. Would it please you?

Clamp the strings down to make all
the joyful chords beckon and bend.
Then, clamp the sky. Then clamp you, in
your death, bleating for notice. Clamp your long
curly hair, that by now is outgrown,
or burned up. Look, in the sky there are cords
for the trees on the ground, there are clouds,
mirror images. There are two coins.
I put one in my pocket. I put one in your hair.
And the coin of the sun I leave there.

THE MOONS OF PLUTO

I don't even know who I am anymore.
Dog at my feet. Sunlamp blasting my face.
Beethoven on headphones. I've never owned
the sun before. Who has? What about a moon of Jupiter?
Io? Calamity? The moons of Uranus are all
Shakespearean characters—tragic dead ladies
and mischievous satyrs. Not one of them named
Fool, though that's Shakespeare's most common
character, the daffy living tarot card who speaks
truth in riddles. I have never owned the sun before
but before I had one son I dreamed another.
Before my son was birthed I dreamt myself a mother,
I dreamed uncovered though in the night
my feet lipped the edge of the blanket
I burrowed into. Here comes another moon
of Saturn though this one's just letters
and numbers—a scientific code—misshapen
satellite, lumpy rock not worth a name.
In my own moony face I see two craters,
I see two eyes. Where are my satellites?
At night I dream I have long hair
and am pregnant again but not worried
about it though if I were pregnant again
I think it would kill me, almost 40,
exhausted, endometriotic, and a year
into a pandemic. What about the moons
of Pluto? Does Pluto have moons? Yes,
and of course they're all named for under-
worldly things. I have a second cousin
named Persephone, who had
the most beautiful long black hair
when we were kids. I coveted that hair,
her beauty. Just a few years older than me,
she orbited her grandmother's house,
dark and mysterious, a can of generic

soda in her hand, then, suddenly
married young and pregnant. What if
she'd gone to the underworld? On that
side of my family everyone has beautiful
black hair but not me. Pluto gets moons.
Our moon doesn't have a name, beyond Moon,
like how my daughter names all her dolls
whatever they are. Her stuffed puppy is Doggie.
All four of her babydolls are Baby.
Is Doggie a girl or a boy? I ask her as I tie
a ribbon around its neck as a leash,
not a noose. She says, No, that's Doggie.
It's the second week of remote classes. A lot
of snow falls and the temp drops.
I sign in to teach to rows of black squares.
Everyone's camera's off, but my students
still want to tell me about their boyfriends,
their mothers, their brothers, their coming out,
they want to talk about feminism, and I love
how teaching like this feels like hosting a call-in
radio program. Though I am tired. My back aches.
My eyes water. Am I alone? I am taking
a lot of medication so I don't cry all the time.
The sun slices off the snow. It is not coming
to catch me nor can I catch it. Before I left
New York state I went to a bar and someone had
graffitied Andrew Marvell's poetry in a bathroom stall—
though we cannot make our sun stand still,
yet we will make him run. It was probably one
of my students—where else would someone
in Potsdam, New York, read metaphysical poetry?
I have never owned the sun. I cannot catch
the wind, though my dog snarls and tries to bite it
when it ruffles her fur. Each morning I wake up.
I put on Rondo a capriccio, Rage Over a Lost Penny.

My son has started bedwetting out of the blue
so there's that to clean up. There's the dog
to let out. My daughter who throws her diaper
in the laundry hamper and I need to catch that
so it doesn't explode in the wash and make a mess.
Good morning, life. I am here. I am taking
a lot of medicine so I don't leave you
one day when I'm sad, when the sun is bully
riding across the sky, fists balled. When my eyes
are all moons, drunk and quartered, halved,
new, named after seasonal activities, look at
them collecting, like pennies, like fish scales,
like neon threads that fall from my children's
socks, like my cousin Persephone collected
beauty, like the real Persephone collected
pomegranate seeds she spit back in her hands
like bitter pills. When the moons come, I will be
in my tunnel in the snow, a child on each side of me,
my dog at my feet—where'd she come from?—
the February air a cold hand pressed against my chest.

A KING HOLDS A CRYSTAL

Let the frolicksome lusty boy
of autumn into the forest
behind my house. Not my real
house, the house I imagine
in the place I grew up,
stacked with beauty and water
I could never afford.
Behind my real house
the cemetery, broken
tree limbs from the storm.
Let's keep the trees out
of this poem. Let's keep the graves
out too and the ticks
riding leaves down to the ground
in the autumn city
full of empty lots
where my son's school
is nestled like an egg.
In autumn the dead come
back, my son says. In autumn
a king holds a crystal
and looks through a dozen
windows and from the twelfth
he can see the wrinkles in
spacetime. Hold my crystal,
my son says as he peers
through his telescope
trying to spy Mars' red
deserts, red as the leaves
in autumn that cover our yard,
covered in ticks, that cover
the graves, that cover the autumn
city, my son's school.
Leaf me alone! my son shouts
as he runs into the leaf pile,

proud of his pun and his speed
and his ability to kick the leaves
in high arcs, like red dust
arcs on the surface of Mars,
I guess—I wouldn't know.
Is there a mischievous boy
is there a satyr, is there a woman
standing naked in the woods
eyes two dead beetles ready
to turn into a bull made of leaves?

REVISION WITH PLAYGROUND AND SEIZURE

We were in the shared space of hello,
the shared persuasive space of goodbye.
The vaulted windows of the kindergarten
overlooked the playground, each child
copying *it* on their own clean sheet
of paper, drawing a scribbled-up tree.
I was holding the baby. I was always
holding the baby. In the trees outside
the sunlight pelted some birds.
My son hid behind my legs.

In the first draft of the day,
there is time, which belongs to everyone.
There's a sergeant sun in the sky
bossing the minutes. My son climbs
into my bed in the morning,
complaining of a sore throat.
One of his cats is dead, but he still
has the other one. He's had
a tummy ache all weekend.

In the second draft, the power
is still on and I'm making
breakfast for both kids, the baby
singing *Ma ma ma* in her highchair,
smearing milk from her sippy cup
into her hair. In the third draft
a beeping alarm shouts *Get up! Get up!*

We are here on the playground,
my husband running to my daughter
as she knocks herself over with a swing.
The sun has come to give us flowers.

The flowers turn into a river, a gust
of wind carrying the autumn chill,
the pulsing nerve in the center of my brain
that once, when I was a child, flipped
and flipped as I convulsed on the floor
in a sun-hot fever. And there were my parents,
for once holding hands with each other,
before the rushed ride to the hospital,
where a doctor stuck a needle in my spine
to test for meningitis, and my father held
my arms down, and my mother cried
in a chair outside the room, unable to watch.

I remember the mystery, like today,
why time stopped but didn't,
the hot crackle of a list of things I'd forget,
that I keep forgetting, like my father's young face
staring back at me, or the time he carried
me on his shoulders all the way over the steel
bridge in the center of town, whistling
a George Thorogood song, the rush
of the cold bay beneath the walkway grating,
the cars speeding by beside us.
We were on our way to see my mother,
who was finishing her shift at a diner.

We must have all smiled when we united,
though I can't remember that, we must have all
clung together, like I do with my kids now,
on the playground, like the sun clung to the sky
when I woke in a strange bed as a child,
and could see the sun driving time forward
through the hospital curtains. Even then,
I knew it was trying to piece something together
that wouldn't work. That's the fourth draft:
the cycling sun, the stranger phantom of the day.

SKELETON KEY VILLANELLE

It's Rondo a Capriccio and Beethoven is angry again.
The piano pounds from the speakers, my son
kicking his legs under the table to the tempo's fast train

which speeds through the living room, fast pain
we can't catch or board, this loaded gun.
It's Rondo a Capriccio and Beethoven is angry again.

He's lost a penny, he's lost many, he's lost his brain.
My son traces a maze with his finger, one
leg kicking under the table to the tempo's fast train.

This was supposed to be a poem with a key, then
a door in which the key would slide, but then
a capricious rounding hit us: Beethoven, angry again.

A rusty iron skeleton key might weigh down
a small boy's pocket. We race the sun,
legs hitching to catch the tempo's fast train.

The music lifts us, a son, a mother. Someone
better close the drapes. We trapse—outrun.
It's Rondo a Capriccio and Beethoven is angry again,
beating each note like an impossible train.

SIMPLE MACHINES

Let dawn come. In the language of sleeplessness
We call it want. We call it heat. I tried to move
The wheel but it wouldn't budge. I tried to turn
The crank, to slide the rope in the pulley's
Smooth groove, its metal gulley. With a mouth
Full of music I spent a fall once studying
Simple machines. The teacher who tried
To grab me in the hall was a lever, maybe,
Was an axle. "Pass the trash" is a phrase
In academia to refer to moving a predator
From one institution to another. You might
Pass the trash with a bucket and dump.
That's not a machine. I made it up.

That's why I was failing 6th grade science.
I just want to talk to you for a minute,
Said the teacher, as he tried to pull me into
His empty classroom, and I ran, bolted down
The hall, crying and scared. How my parents
Had to come in for a meeting but he didn't
Lose his job. How I got moved to another class.
How he said I looked so much like my aunt
Who had been such a good girl twenty years earlier.
Now he's surely dead because I am forty,
And then he was already middle aged.

Now, it's the hottest summer on record.
All the memes say it's the coolest summer
We'll ever see again. Both things are true.
This is profound in the age of memes.
The world is burning, is cooking, is boiling,
Is giving itself an acid ocean bath.
The temperature spikes to a hundred on the rim
Of Lake Michigan, again, again, tho it is June.
The air conditioner goes out. I sweat in bed

With my children, my husband, as pain laces
Through my pelvis, my left hip a surgeon would like
To enter with a mechanical arm and scalpel,
To remake in the image of something holier.

There is a difference between kinetic
And potential energy, though both are found
In simple machines. In a screw, bearing down
To hold a thing in place, harnessing its brass
Spirals. You could put the screws to someone,
To a person, a hot body, to my hip.
On an incline plane, you could roll a boulder
Down, like Sisyphus, when he loses his grip,
When he slips. And in a wedge, like an axe,
To split apart, as dawn splits cool night
From morning, as dusk splits blister hot day
From evening, as an axe could cut
An arm off, as an axe could cut an arm
As it reaches for an eleven-year-old girl,
Insisting, *I get to touch her.*

ORCHID

I wanted to curl like a seed pod,
caught on a wind in a storm.
Or dropped in a field full of iron,
old factory gone back to meadow,
to weed, or a bog. Or a fungal
laced branch of a half rotten tree.
I wanted to land there and spark,
to sprout a thin stem, a delicate
flower I'd pose for the clouds.

From my flat belly I'd grow
an open and rounded out pouch,
a slipper to catch the small bugs
that, drawn to my colorful face,
lost their weak footing and fell.
A pouch like a well with no water.
A pouch like a paper cup crumpled.

A pouch where I cover with pollen
the gnats and small ants that I catch
and maybe a bee who has wandered
too far from the hive, who has left
her mother alone in a fortress
of hexes and honey that drips
down in gold globules by mother's
rich egg brood, the larvae who'll squirm
forth soon and will feast on the pollen
procured by the wayward young drone
whom they'll one day replace, but not yet.

Remember the flower? The orchid.
Her bright face is waiting, her whiskers
that tickle the cool evening air,
her lavender spots, and her ghostly
green skin, her long pistil, squat stamen.

Her form in pastels, like a drawing,
a sketch that holds loosely together
unless a child's hand comes to brush
away the hard work and the color,
unless a strong light makes it fade.

But not the wild orchid. In the swamp,
the field, in the ditch, on the shore,
the pebble strewn shore of an ancient
lake, on some weather worn drift wood
the orchid grows, dressed like the dawn.

ELEGY WITH LAND BRIDGE

for Dean Young

Death happens and we all have to keep going.
Remember writing? I don't. When my teacher died
I remembered his collection of embroidered shirts,
each thread a river to his heart. I remembered
his dance moves, each jerk of his arms
a line break. I remembered the way he ran
through town, faster, faster, though surely
his heart was already on the way to failing,
surely he was on his way to a new heart,
his feet hurrying the pavement. Let's think about
eyeballs or crazy shapes. About Dadaism.
About Kenneth Koch. Let's think about Keats,
whose manic highs and lows fascinated
my teacher, who my teacher even looked like!
Now that I've put an exclamation mark
in my poem, this is a real elegy to my teacher,
who I will never see again. This is a real elegy
to the landscape of soft rolling hills that edge
dramatically into limestone cliffs when they hit
the river. This is a real elegy for a small rock
painted with green swirls that somebody left
on my desk. I couldn't see the edge of the cliff
or the river or the rock. I could only see
my teacher, at the front of the classroom
gesticulating wildly as he quoted Hopkins,
each quote an ecstasy, each movement
of his arms a splash of sprung verse,
and every time he pushed his glasses back
up his nose bridge—a little goodbye.
There, there are two people on a bridge,
on a land bridge at the edge of a river,
and one of them is stopping in the middle
and turning around to take a last look
at the trumpet vines blasting their blossoms
in the late August fog, and at the hills, and at us.

BEAR BAITING WITH ANNE BOLEYN

Bait the old blind bear
        if you want. It will only bellow,
    discontent, will only maul every
    particle of air, will turn its head
        left to right around, its eyes
            round pupil plates searching satellites,
looking for the dogs it can't see
    but wants to bite, the dogs
whose necks it wants to snap
    between its velveteen teeth.
    Let's keep the dogs out
            of the night crinkled forest
        chasing the bull's soft hide
            chasing an enemy only dogs can see
            only dogs can smell
        only dogs can touch
        like a blank new moon
    invisible in the sky, black hole punched
        through the tin foil firmament
            spat through with planets.
    A man holds a wooden rod
        jealous swans hissing
            river plastic beneath their feet
    the trees a cacophony of insects
        the dogs yowling. The bear
circles the man and his rod
    the man beating the bear's haunches
        handprint choking the neck
            of the rod. The bear growls as leaves
            cascade down around him
            red and dank smelling.
                The bear is a far away
        tourniquet she has sent to stop
    the bleeding, to kill the man
            in the trees with the dogs.

She is the bull goring tree bark
with her sturdy horns
smearing them with the man's
warm blood. Is this historically accurate?
I guess I wouldn't know why
it would matter when history
is a fable, is a parable,
is a king peering through a twelfth window
to stare at the naked woman,
to mumble, Her head is mine.

ROCK CYCLE

Remember fire. The one in
the Earth's molten core, in its lead rich
combustible heart. In my own heart—
a murmur, a wobbling beaten
out rhythm that pulls me from sleep,
from the dream where I run from a woman's
gnarled hand, to a cry that unbuckles
the dog from her mat.

Recall the erosion of gullies,
of sandstone and limestone,
of dirt from the fields and the lawns to
the creeks, to the streams, the old rivers
that dent the Earth's mantle, that weaken
its plates just a bit, not a fault line,
a pucker, a kiss. The rock dust moves, rushes
in rivers that push the silt out to
the sea, to the ocean, to settle
in trenches, the edge of one plate
and another, a chasm to grind
the silt under the mantle, to melt
into magma, to erupt and ooze out
into tubes of new rock, to restart the whole cycle.

A fireplace, hot, in a house has a mantle.
I could line it with knick-knacks, with dried herbs
and tokens, with portraits of children
and weddings, with prayer cards from funerals—
my grandmother's face staring back.
She is not a stalactite, no calcium
drip, though her bones will recycle
one day in a million or two million
years, as this mantle will buckle,
will fold and reshape and transform.

How once the Earth froze for a million
cold years, but then thawed, how it wobbled
away from the sun, how its atmosphere
thinned, how it warmed, how its continents
spread. How its winds and its rains formed
a butte, formed a dell, formed a person,
adamic, to name all the rivers
she saw, to gobble the fishes
and bring forth a planet of people.

Is this the old woman I see in
my dream? In my dream she is screeching.
Her teeth make a whistle, some staticky
sound, like a plate sliding under
another plate down in the ocean,
like the world that keeps churning its rocks,
nothing wasted, all used, in the end.

PASTEL

When I was an ignorant child
I stared in the face of glory
or was it the face of my mother
holding open a book of art prints
to say *Look, look,* though we
were poor, too poor for art.
When you are too poor for art,
you cannot afford anything
even the truth. The truth is I loved
my mother and her pastels,
which she kept in a leather case,
and her special paper I wasn't
allowed to touch. It was a different
time then we could afford to live
in our own town. Not like now
when everybody lives in an apartment
complex on the edge of town
so vacationers can buy
all the shitty little bungalows.
In the streets, no children
are riding bicycles, or walking
to the schools, which have been
torn down, and the park is full
of moneyed retirees, who've turned
the beach into a bird refuge,
so no children are swimming there
or making sandcastles. The way wealth
chews through everything pretty,
pries open your hand, like a mother
pries open the hand of her child,
and says *You give that back to me right now.*

STORM SONNET

We rushed to shut the windows when the storm
raced thru the woods, the lightning bolt that forked
outside the open door, the wind forlorn
and angry, beating its fists until it worked
some branches from the trees, the bay a stirred-
up bowl I couldn't see the bottom of.
I screamed when a bolt shot near us, when the waves turned
to white hands that slapped each other
to the rocky shore, when the air unhooked
its golden mask and showed its bone rich face.
There is the afterlife, the room we tried to book,
the molecules depleted, lightless space
where atoms spin themselves into fine threads
to weave a tapestry of worlds unsaid.

FLOWERS WITH ANNE BOLEYN

I saw the days and then the hours
sprouting like wheeled hallucinations
off the tidal river that cut
the dirty city through its core.
Even the river swans flew away
angry and hissing, heads barely attached.
In memory I saw my daughter
counting her toes in French and Latin
the blue veins on her feet showing
blood ghosts through her skin.
I saw her leaving as time leaves
ticking and scattering little finger bones,
moss and lichen, small maggots
that chew the walnut's green skin
the earthy cushion that hides
its hard nut. If a rift in the earth
should happen, if thunder rolls
around the throne,
if the blood of the day washes
out of the courtyard and
drains into the river, the same river
that splits this bad tooth city.
These blossoms, I don't know 'em,
dangling flirtatiously, not like open pussies,
I guess, more like upside down jester hats
spangled with virtuous wool balls,
ready to amuse or be cast off, just as
ready to give pleasure for only one day.
In my head, in my memory, I can see
the glassless window. It is really just a hole
through a wall to the outside air,
rotten and brisk, strawfilled. Barefoot,
the shoeless executioner danced, did dance,
did reckon, did reap, did unhead the air
tight around my neck.

NOTES

The villanelles in this collection were written as interlocking pairs, so that the third stanza of the first villanelle in each pair is the first stanza of the second, though they do not appear in that order in this collection. If you are interested in reading them that way, however, here is a key. "Manufactured Autumn Leaf Holiday Wreath Villanelle" and "Paper Skeleton Villanelle" are a pair; "Skeleton Key Villanelle" and "Train Villanelle" are a pair. "Unmoored Villanelle" has a pair, but it is not included here.

Several poems in this collection were originally written as contrapuntals, then pulled apart into separate poems. If you are interested in reading them as contrapuntals, here is a key (the first poem in each pairing should be placed to the left of the second). "A Dozen Sons" and "A Dozen Daughters" pair together; "Your Last Autumn" and "Cat Costume" pair together; "Two Lovers" and "Two Dogs" pair together; "Blue" and "Flowers with Anne Boleyn" pair together; "Blood Moon" and "Bog Body" pair together; "A King Holds a Crystal" and "Bear Baiting with Anne Boleyn" pair together.

"The Sweating Sickness," from which the title of this book is taken, references a mysterious plague that repeatedly struck northern France and England in the sixteenth century. The disease was swift and often fatal; victims either recovered or died within twenty-four hours. Like Covid-19, one infection did not provide immunity. People could repeatedly contract the illness.

"Flowers with Anne Boleyn" references the line *"circa Regna tonat,"* from Thomas Wyatt's poem *"Innocentia Veritas Viat Fides Circumdederunt me inimici mei."* Wyatt composed the poem from the Tower of London, where he was imprisoned in 1536 on suspicion of having an affair with Anne Boleyn, and after witnessing the executions of Anne Boleyn and her five accused "lovers," including her brother, George Boleyn. Wyatt was Boleyn's childhood friend and neighbor, and, though he had made advances toward her before her marriage to Henry VIII, there is no evidence to suggest that the two had a sexual relationship. Additionally, most historians today agree that Anne Boleyn was innocent of all charges against her, including of adultery, incest, and treason. Wyatt was the only person accused of sleeping with Boleyn who was not executed. *Circa Regna tonat* translates to "thunder rolls around the throne."

ACKNOWLEDGMENTS

Grateful acknowledgement is made to the editors of the following publications, in which these poems first appeared:

Allium, A Journal of Poetry & Prose ("Revision with Suicide and Ogres"); *American Poetry Review* ("Abortion Poem," "Orchid"); *Anti-Heroine Chic* ("Pastel"); *Beloit Poetry Journal* ("Salt Marsh Moth"); *Bennington Review* (Train Villanelle," "Skeleton Key Villanelle"); *Cherry Tree* ("Blue"); *Cincinnati Review* ("Exit"); *Copper Nickel* ("Paper Skeleton Villanelle," "Unmoored Villanelle"); *Harvard Review Online* ("Nothing"); *Juked* ("The Underworld"); *Kenyon Review* ("Ablation"); *Massachusetts Review* ("In Morning," "Get Lost Serenade"); *Miracle Monocle* ("Moses"); *Missouri Review* ("Specter," "Chariot," "Night Elegy," "The Sweating Sickness," "Inquisition," "Predictive Models," "Flowers with Anne Boleyn"); *Mumbermag* ("Noose"); *New England Review* ("A Dozen Daughters," "The Red Planet"); *Nimrod International Journal* ("Cabin"); *Northwest Review* ("The Moons of Pluto"); *Pleiades* ("Mule"); *Poet Lore* ("When the Wind Blows"); *Poetry Northwest* ("A Dozen Sons," "Your Last Autumn"); *Prairie Schooner* ("Revision with Playground and Seizure"); *Seneca Review* ("Leda"); *Southern Review* ("Two Lovers," "Bog Body"); *Threepenny Review* ("Elegy with Land Bridge"); and *Waxwing* ("Nike, Medusa, Jocasta, Split"). Thanks as well to *Verse Daily* for reprinting "Paper Skeleton Villanelle," "Train Villanelle" and "Skeleton Key Villanelle."

Thank you to Terrance Hayes, Nancy Krygowski, and Jeffrey McDaniel for selecting *The Sweating Sickness* for inclusion in the Pitt Poetry Series, and for your generous editorial feedback.

Thank you to Saint Mary's College in Indiana, whose CFAI summer grants provided financial support so that I could finish this book.

All of the villanelles in this collection, as well as the poems "Leda," "Orchid," and "Rock Cycle" were written in online poetry workshops offered by Annie Finch in 2021 and 2022. Thank you, Annie, for helping me see how the line rocks.

Thank you to the poets and writers whose feedback, support, mentorship and friendship helped me write, edit and think through these poems: Melissa Ginsburg, Sandra Simonds, Marc Rahe, Diane Seuss, Erika Meitner, Catherine Cafferty, Cole Swensen, Barbara Hamby, MC Hyland, Sugi Ganeshananthan, Joyelle McSweeney, James Hall, Jo Luloff and Kathryn Nuernberger. Thanks to Oliver de la Paz, aureleo sans, A. Rafael Johnson, and KC Mead-Brewer, who sat on an AWP panel called "Writing the Monster" with me in Seattle in 2023, that pushed me to think more deeply about ideas of the "monster" and the fairytale that are present in this collection. Thank you, as well, to the students in my Fabulism, Fairytale and Fable course at Saint Mary's College in 2023, whose deep engagement and fantastical writing did the same. Thanks to Jimin Seo, Caely McHale, and Reuben Gelley Newman, my co-editors at *Couplet Poetry*, for the ongoing discussions of what a poem is, and what a poem can do.

Thank you to my friends and family: my parents Deb and Jeff Zich and Steve and Holly Lehmann, and my dear friends Andrea D'Agosto and Jennifer Corroy Porras. Thank you to my in-laws Chris and Paul Schuette, and in particular to my father-in-law, Phil Frye, who drove from Michigan to Indiana each week for a full academic year during the pandemic lockdown to watch my children so that I could work. Thanks to my aunt and uncle, Polly and Tom Hobart, for letting me use their cottage in Door County each summer, ostensibly to vacation, but where I always end up writing poems.

And, most of all, thank you to my husband, Josh Frye, whose love and care sustain me, and my children, Asa and Zephyr. I love you forever.